Alien Adventures

Max's Box

Tony Bradman • Jonatronix

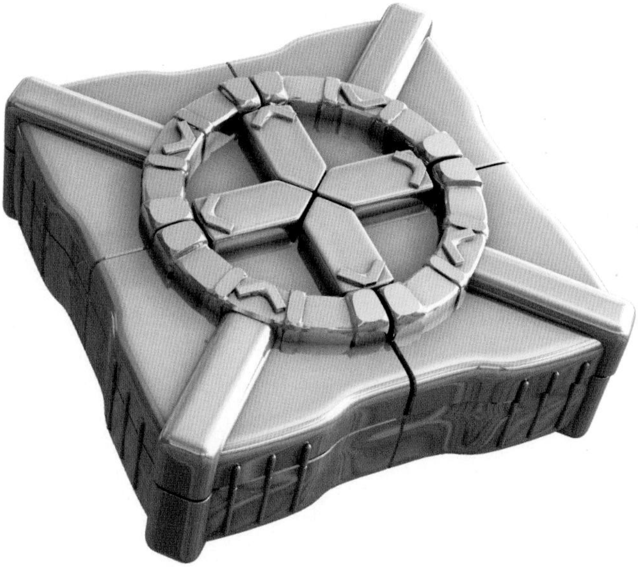

OXFORD
UNIVERSITY PRESS

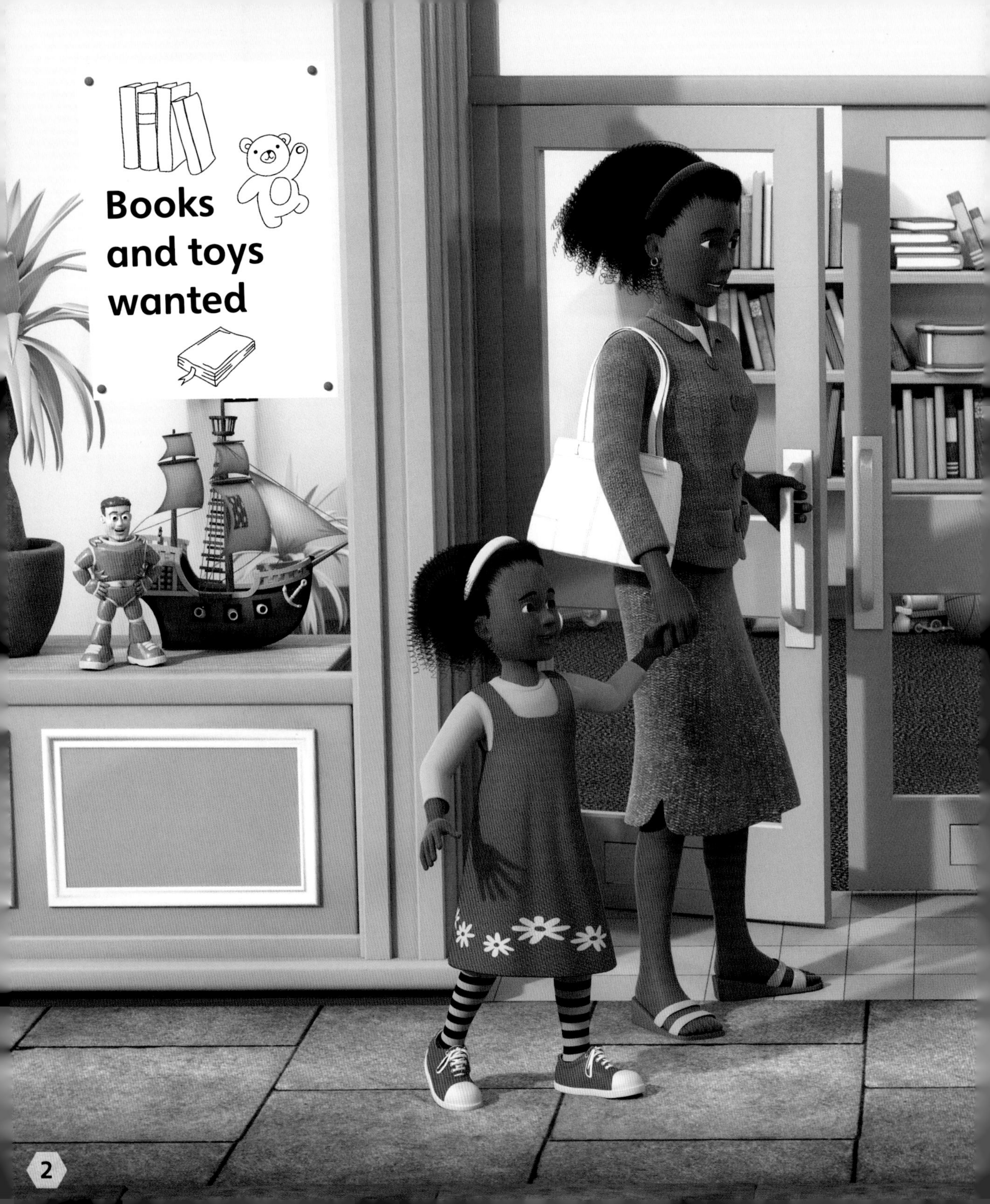
Books
and toys
wanted

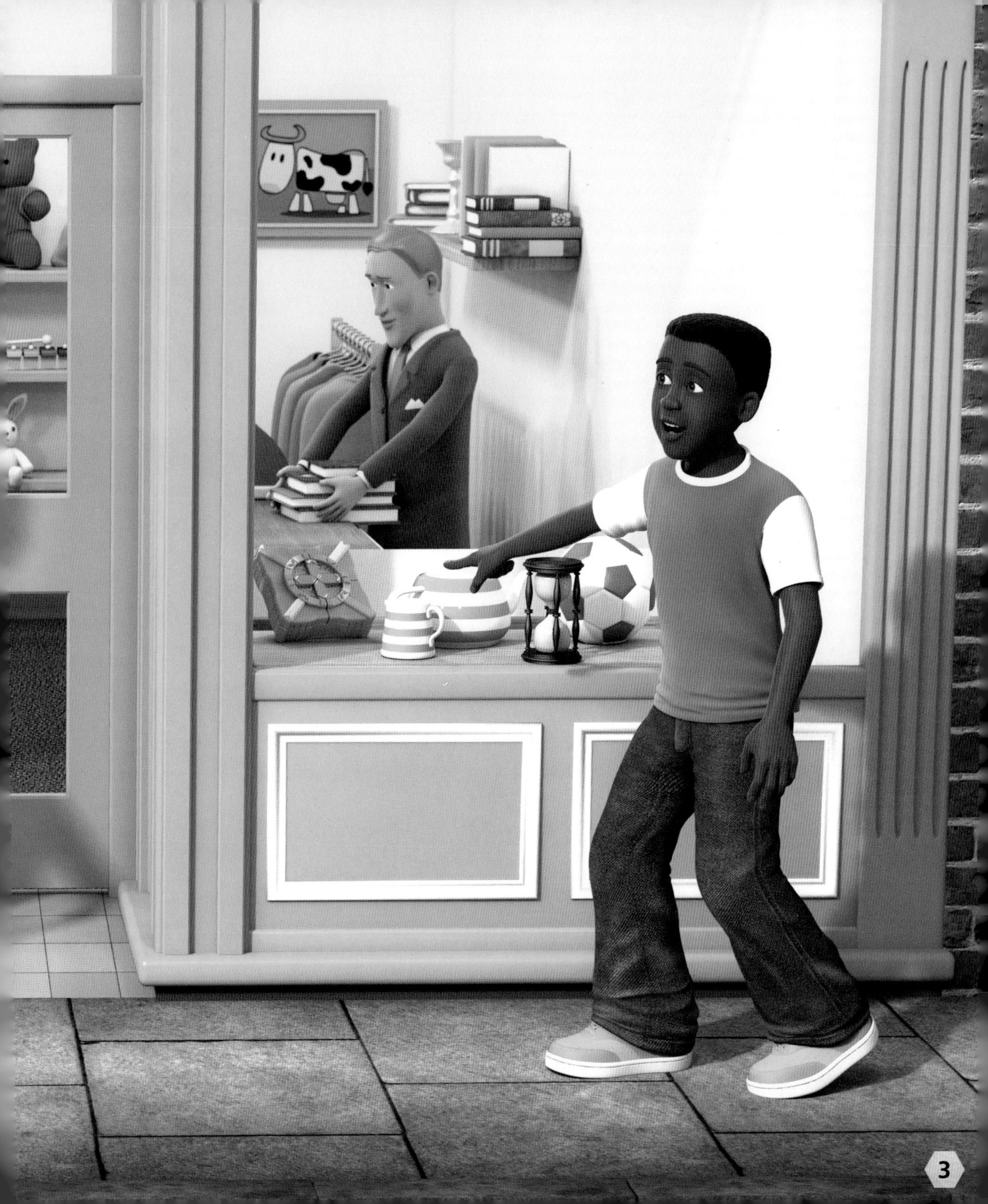

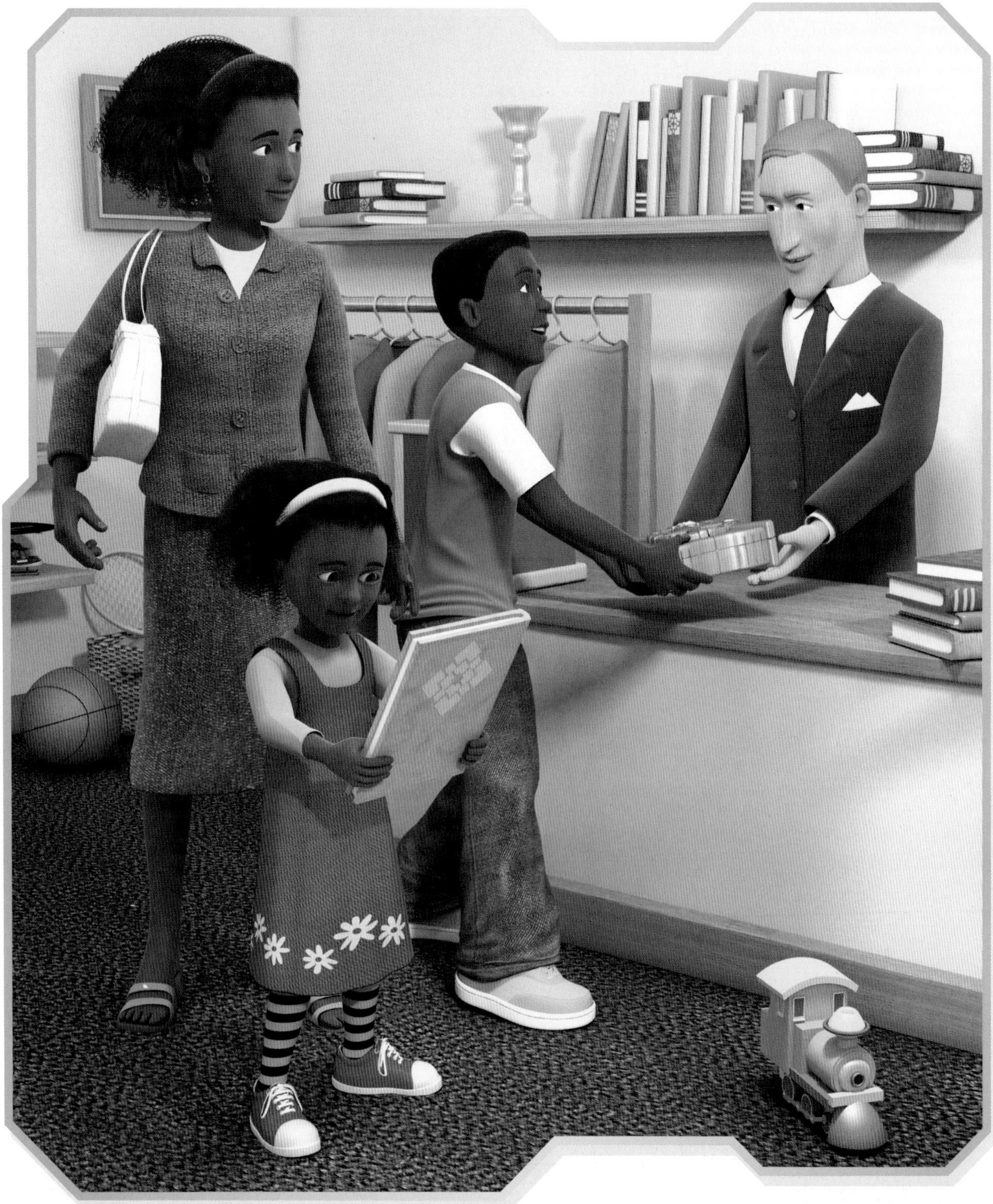

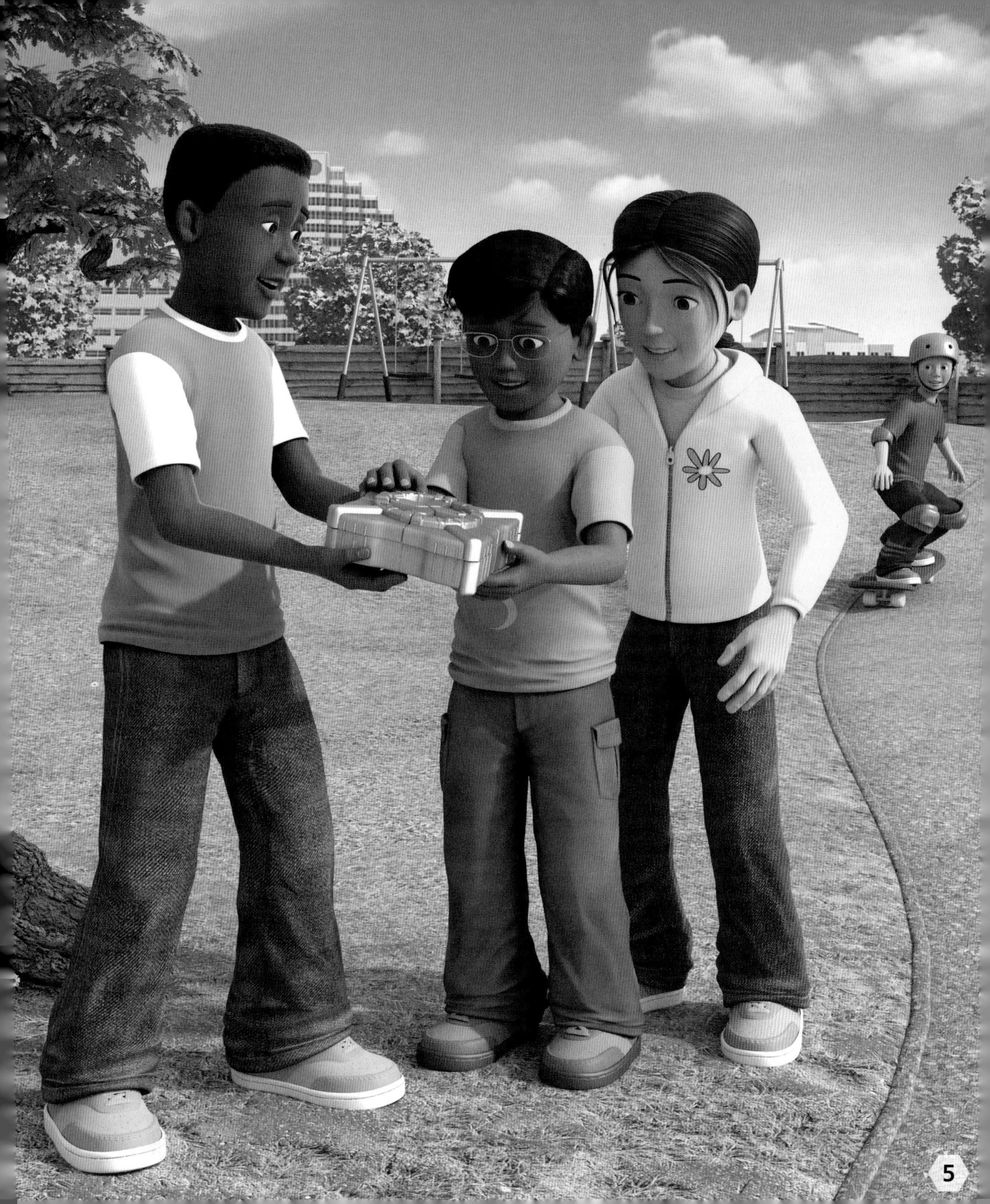

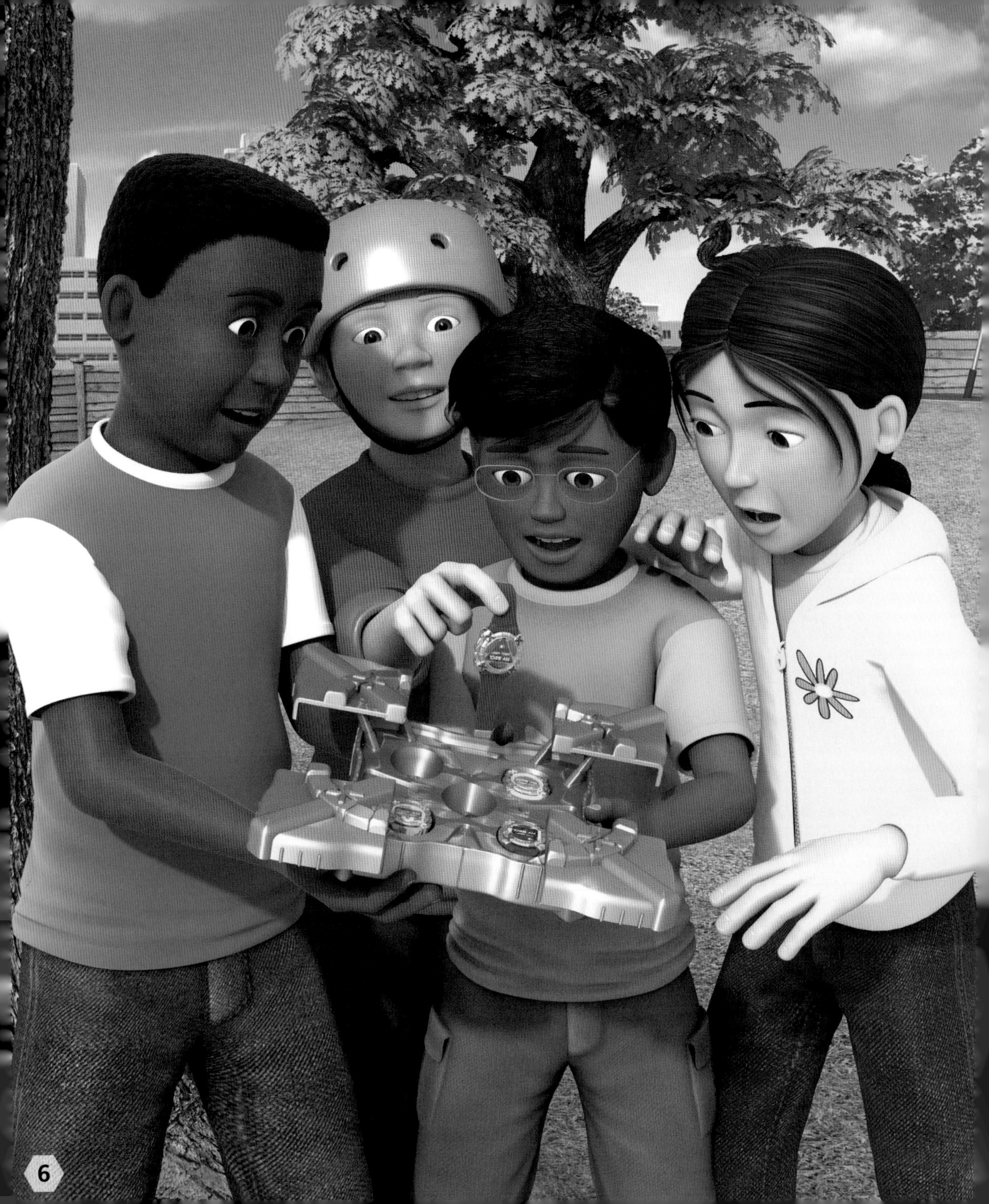

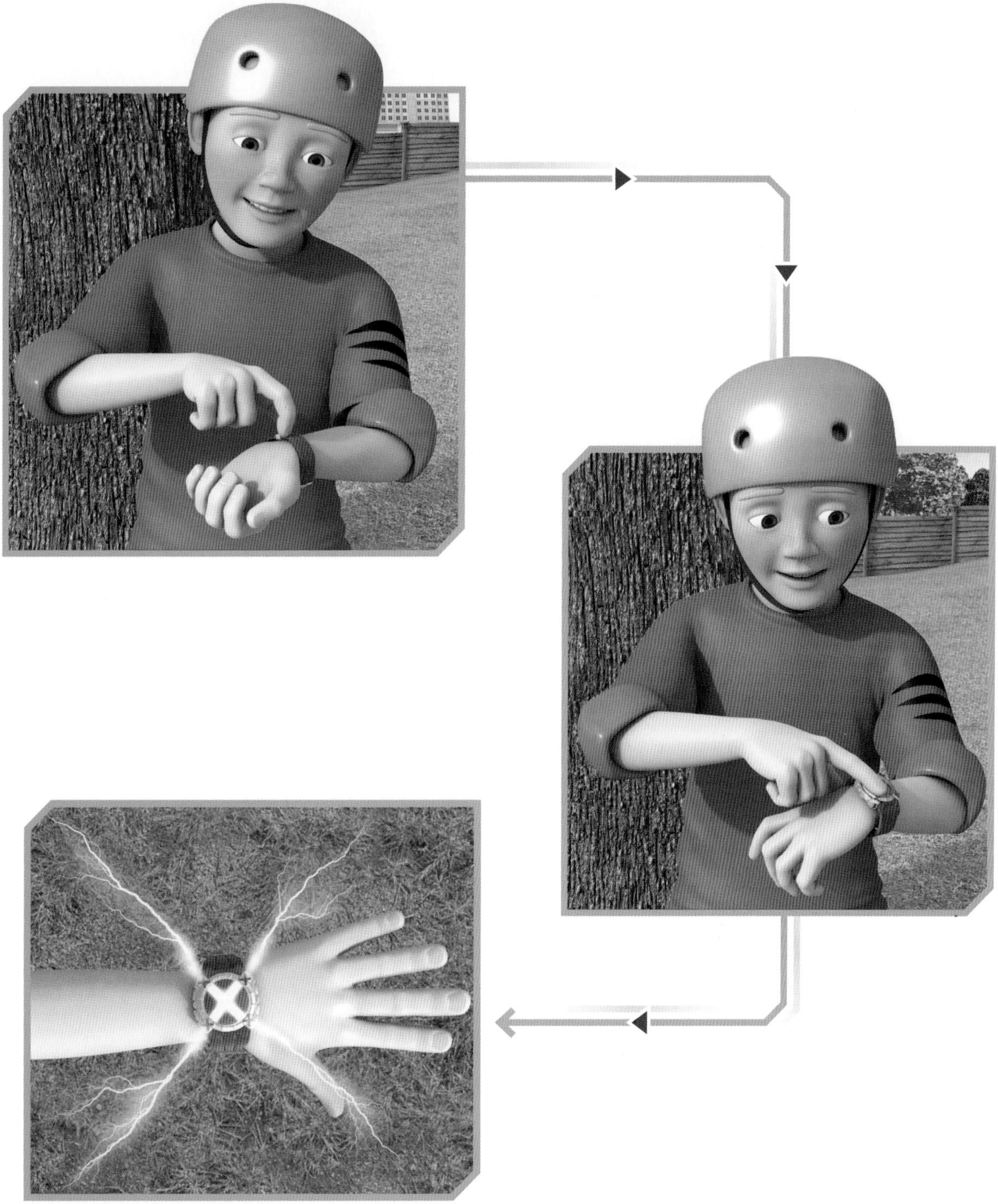

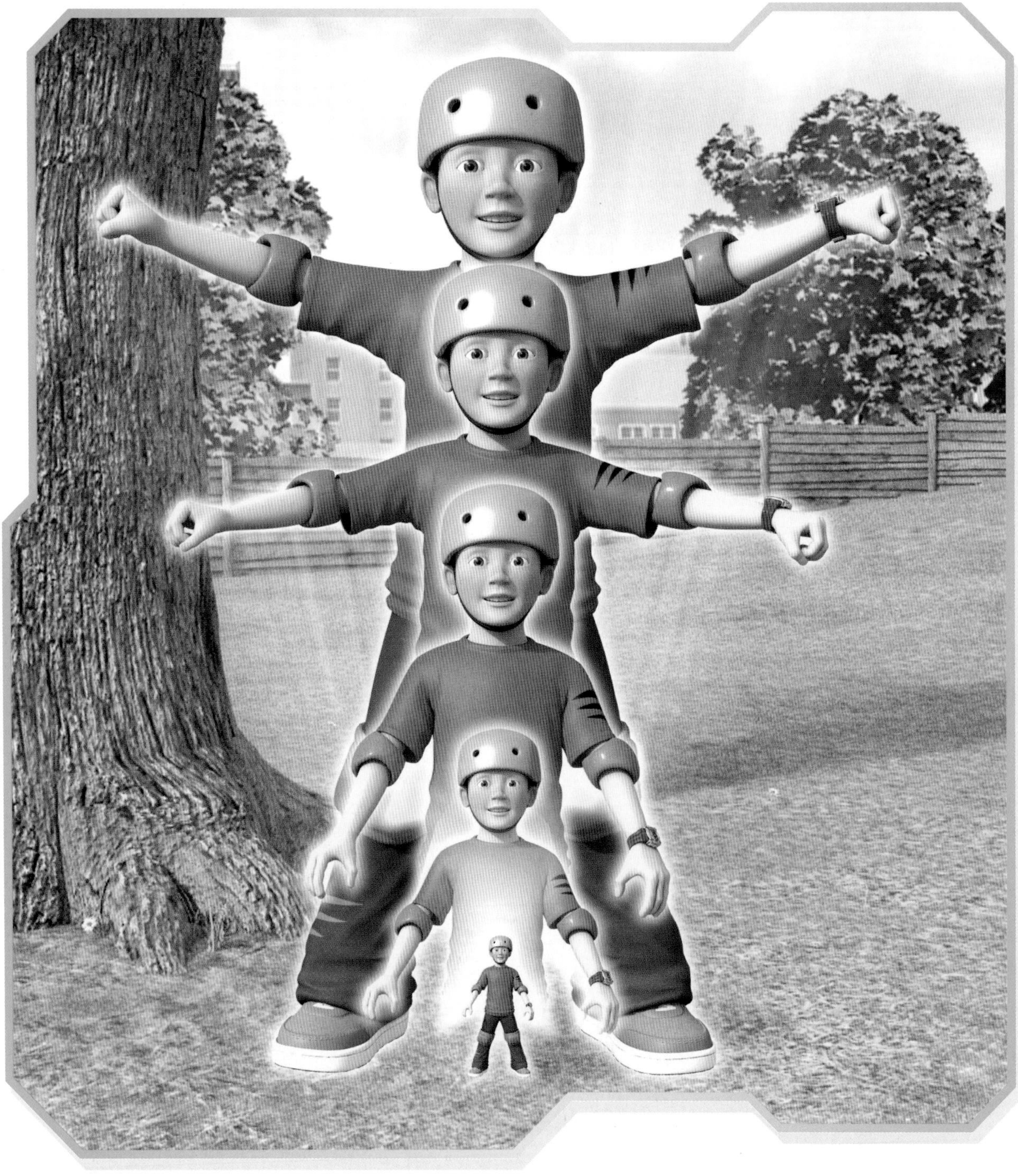

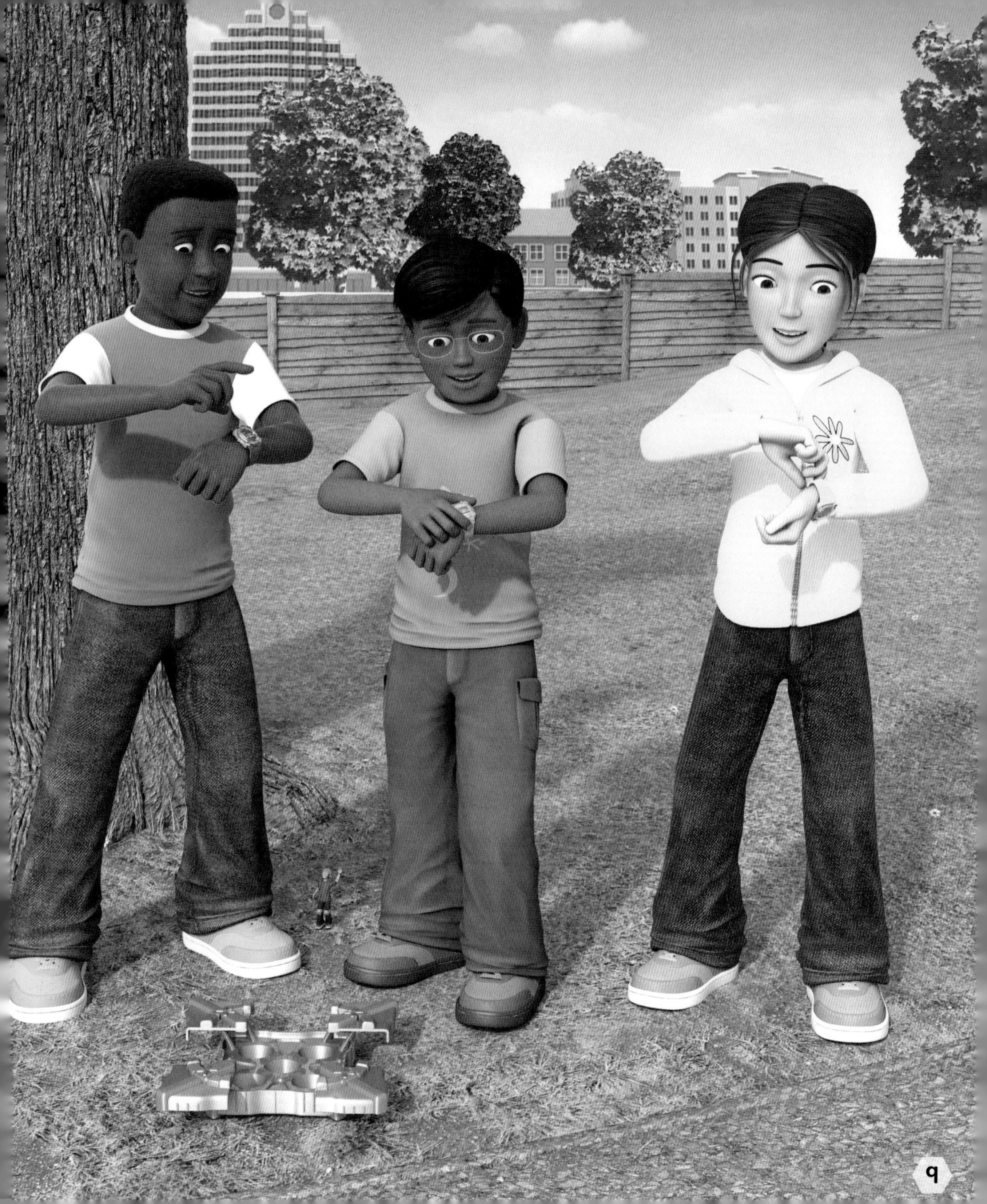

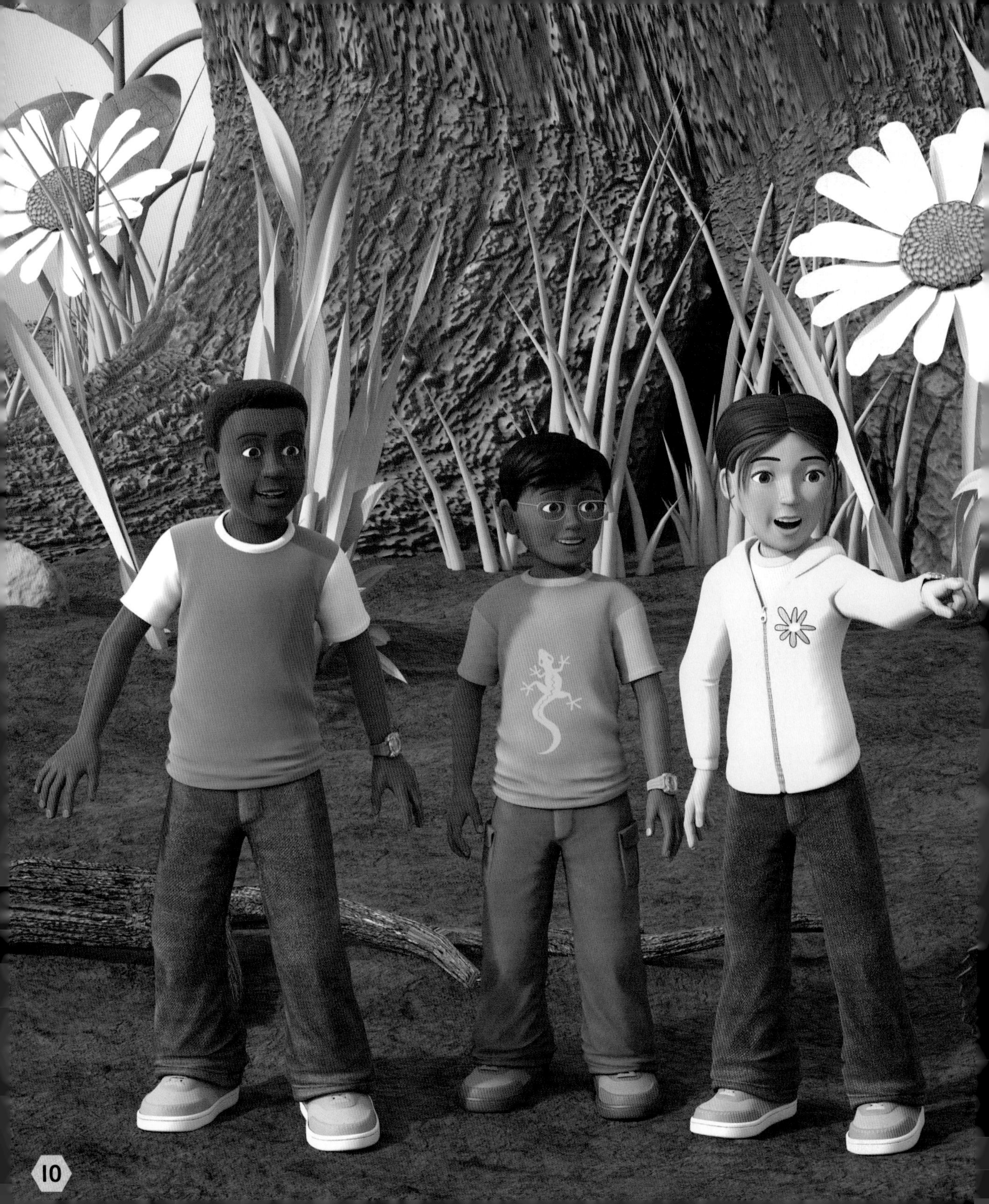

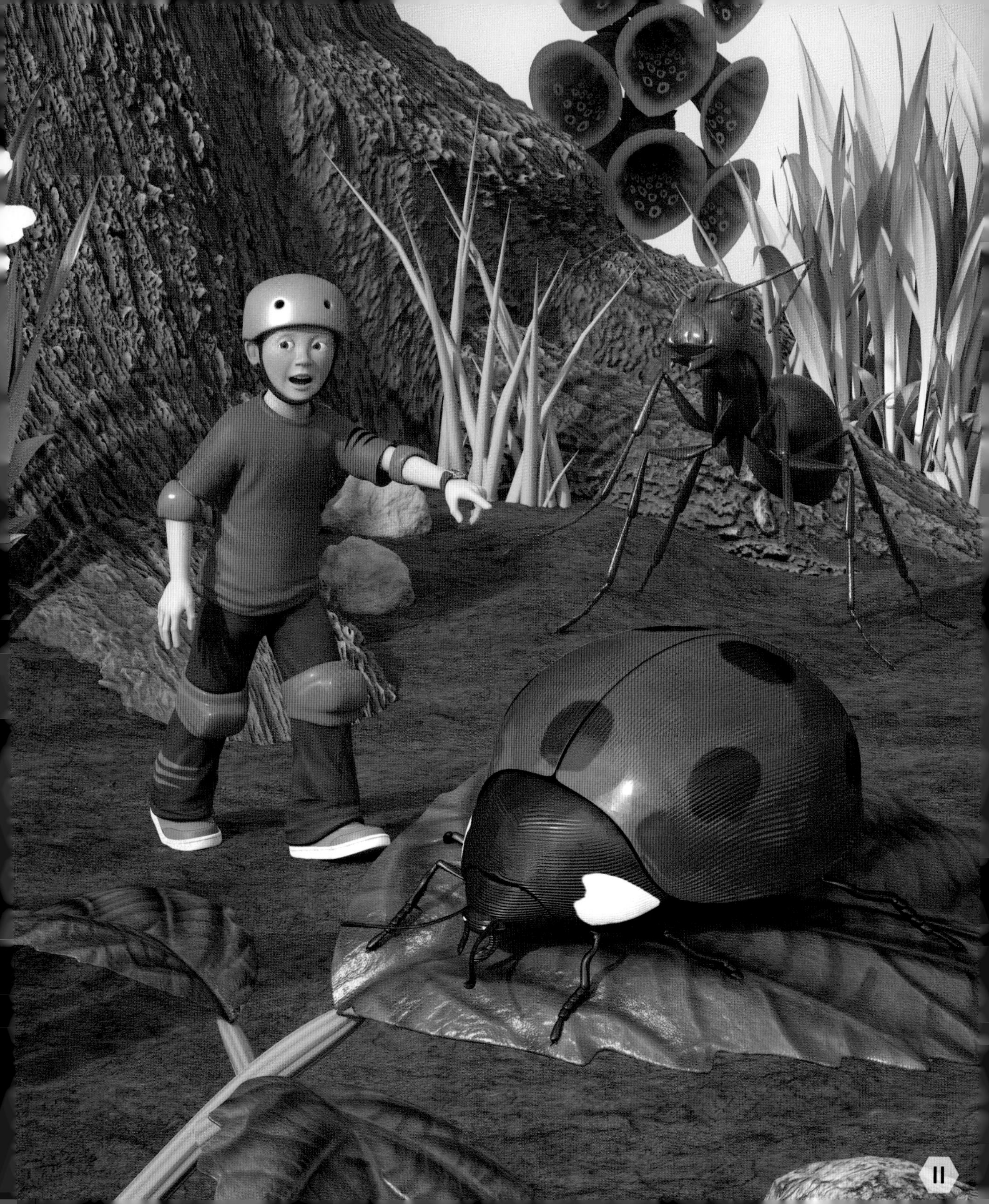

Retell the story

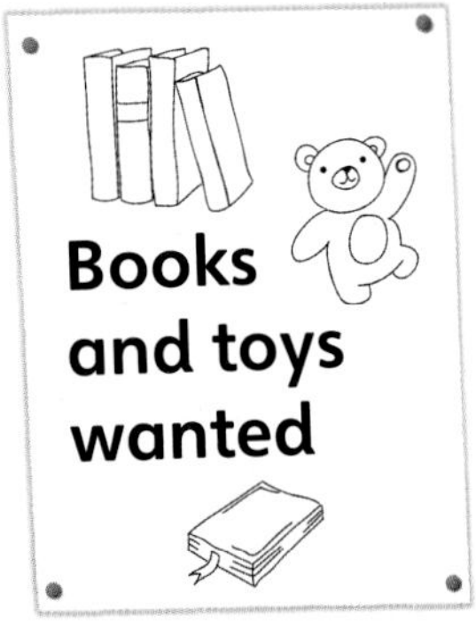

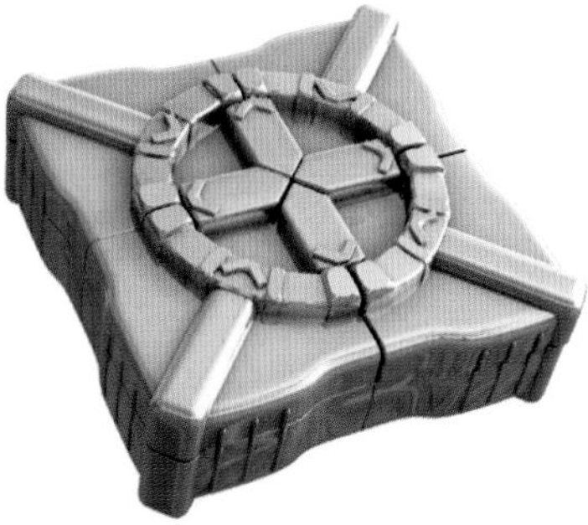

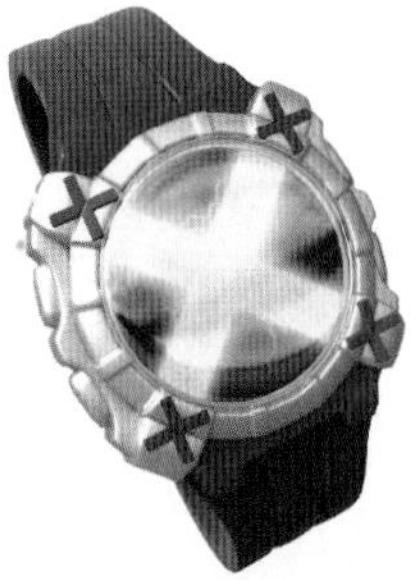

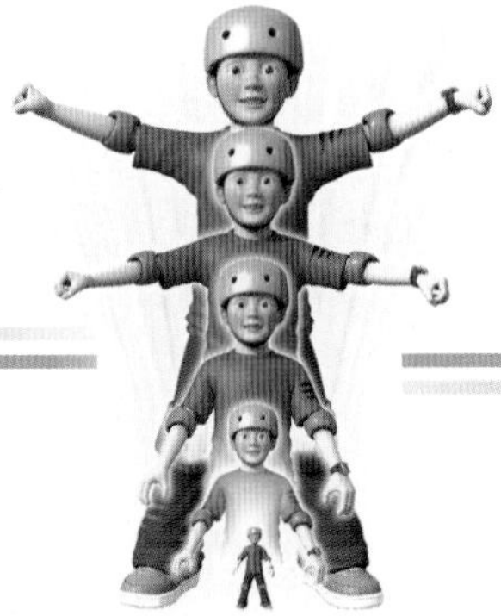

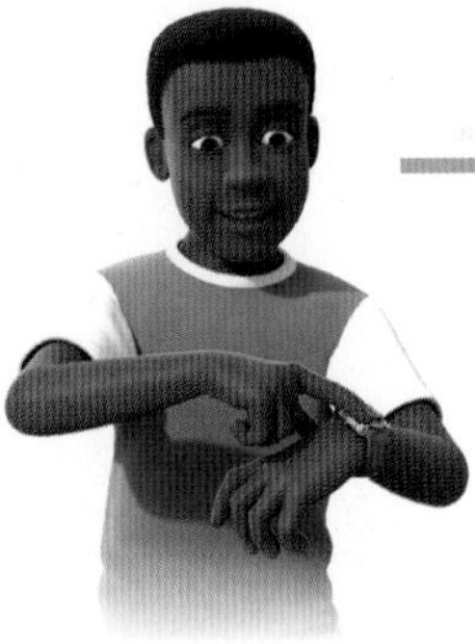

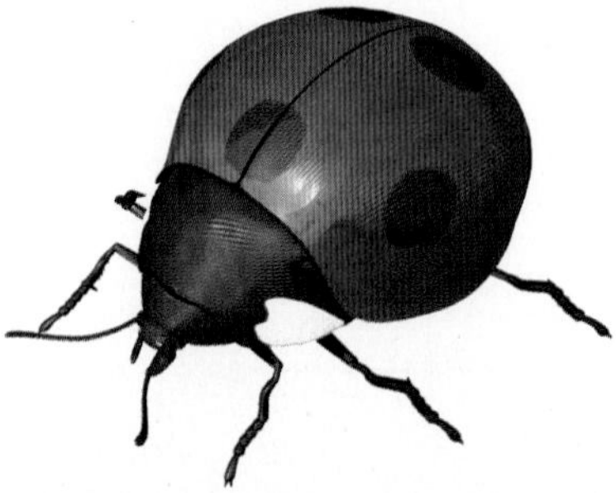